Monster Max's BIG Breakfast

By Dee Reid

Reading Consultant: Beth Walker Gambro

Ruby Tuesday Books

Published in 2018 by Ruby Tuesday Books Ltd.

Design and illustrations: Emma Randall
Editor: Ruth Owen
Production: John Lingham

Library of Congress Control Number: 2018946143
Print (hardback) ISBN 978-1-78856-048-1
Print (paperback) ISBN 978-1-78856-068-9
eBook ISBN 978-1-78856-049-8

Printed and published in the United States of America.

For further information including rights and permissions requests, please contact our Customer Services Department at 877-337-8577.

Max was hungry.

Max ate one red tractor.

Max ate two trees.

I am still hungry.

Max ate three pizzas.

He ate four flowers.

Max ate five pairs of underpants.

He ate six socks.

13

Max ate seven hot dogs.

Max ate eight ants.

Max ate nine balls.

He ate ten doughnuts.

Stop! Stop! Stop!

Max stopped.
Out came a big burp.

BURP!

20

Yuk!

21

Can you match the numbers to the objects?

1 2 3 4 5

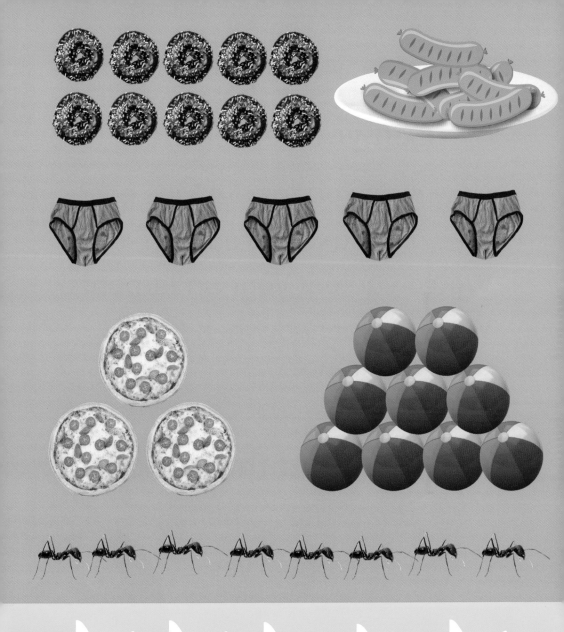

6 7 8 9 10

Can you remember?

How many pizzas did Max eat?

Why did Max keep eating?

Would you eat your underpants?

What happened when Max ate everything?

Can you read these words?

am   ate   he

I   stop   yes